CHINESE COOKING

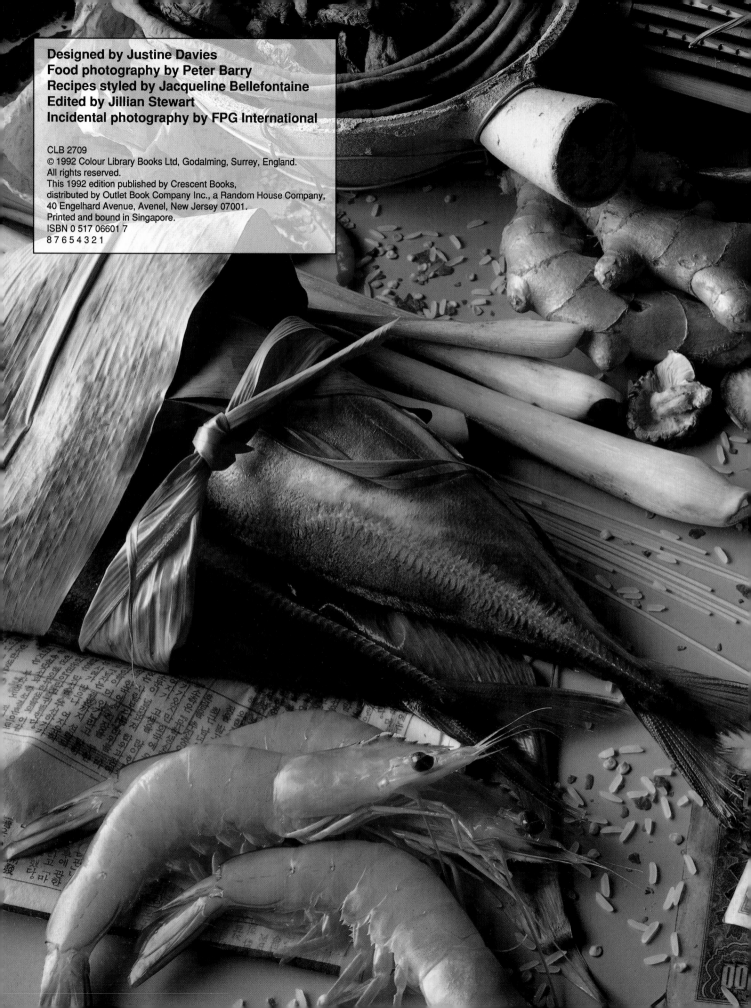

Designed by Justine Davies
Food photography by Peter Barry
Recipes styled by Jacqueline Bellefontaine
Edited by Jillian Stewart
Incidental photography by FPG International

CLB 2709
© 1992 Colour Library Books Ltd, Godalming, Surrey, England.
All rights reserved.
This 1992 edition published by Crescent Books,
distributed by Outlet Book Company Inc., a Random House Company,
40 Engelhard Avenue, Avenel, New Jersey 07001.
Printed and bound in Singapore.
ISBN 0 517 06601 7
8 7 6 5 4 3 2 1

CHINESE COOKING

CRESCENT BOOKS
NEW YORK • AVENEL, NEW JERSEY

INTRODUCTION

Chinese cuisine is one of world's most ancient styles of cooking, yet it has captured modern tastes with its style and simplicity. Western interest in Chinese cuisine came about relatively recently with the first Chinese immigrants who took their enticing recipes to the four corners of the world. In the United States, the earliest Chinese "restaurants" were simply kitchens established to feed the immigrant population, but as word spread, Americans began to discover the delights of Chinese food.

It is rather misleading, though, to talk about Chinese food as if it had one distinct identity. A country as vast as China encompasses a whole range of geographical, climatic and social conditions that lead to various regional styles of cooking. Southern, or Cantonese, cooking is perhaps the style most widely known in the West. The climate is warm and the meals light; stir-fried dishes of crisp vegetables and subtle sauces are characteristic, and rice is the staple accompaniment. In the north wheat is the major crop, therefore noodles are eaten more than rice. The region can be very cold, and rich sauces and meat dishes, as well as dumplings and pancakes, add much needed warmth.

The cuisine of western China is presently enjoying great popularity. Szechuan is a mountainous region famous for its peppercorns and chilies, and its cuisine utilizes these ingredients to create dishes that are pungent and highly spiced. By contrast, eastern China is blessed with a plentiful and varied harvest, which it uses to create dishes that combine the simplicity of northern cuisine with the creative talents of southern chefs.

There are certain characteristics which are common to all these styles of cooking and form the basis of Chinese cuisine. The use of the stir-frying technique is commonplace. The ingredients are carefully cut up into the appropriate shapes to facilitate quick cooking, then fried in a little oil at a high temperature. The secret of successful stir-frying is good preparation and adding the ingredients in the correct order so that the finished dish retains all the taste, goodness and texture of each ingredient.

Texture is something that is very important to the Chinese, who insist that vegetables retain their "bite," and they will often add ingredients that have very little taste but add a nice texture. Dried ingredients are important for this purpose, and many of them, such as dried mushrooms, also have a wonderful flavor. Possibly the most popular attribute of Chinese cooking, and one that makes it eminently suitable for everyday meals, is the short cooking time of most recipes. A wok is the best tool for this purpose, but a deep non-stick pan will serve the purpose.

Chinese cooking is popular because it requires so little in the way of expertise and equipment, yet it offers endless variety and taste. So try a taste of Chinese cooking and you will find China's most delicious dishes can easily be prepared without leaving your own kitchen.

Right: the Imperial Palace in Peking is one China's most symbolic buildings. Ordinary Chinese citizens were once banned from even approaching the so-called Forbidden City.

Wonton Soup

Preparation Time: 25-30 minutes **Cooking Time:** 5-10 minutes **Serves:** 6-8

Probably the best-known Chinese soup, this recipe uses pre-made wonton wrappers for ease of preparation.

Ingredients

20-24 wonton wrappers
½ cup finely minced chicken or pork
2 tbsps chopped cilantro
3 green onions, finely chopped
1 inch piece fresh ginger,
   peeled and grated

1 egg, lightly beaten
5 cups chicken stock
1 tbsp dark soy sauce
Dash sesame oil
Salt and pepper
Cilantro or watercress for garnish

Place all the wonton wrappers on a large, flat surface. Mix together the chicken or pork, chopped cilantro, green onions and ginger. Brush the edges of the wrappers lightly with beaten egg. Place a small mound of mixture on one half of the wrappers and fold the other half over the top to form a triangle. Press with the fingers to seal the edges well.

    Bring the stock to the boil in a large saucepan. Add the filled wontons and simmer 5-10 minutes or until they float to the surface. Add remaining ingredients to the soup, using only the leaves of the cilantro or watercress for garnish.

The bright lights of the Jumbo floating restaurant in Hong Kong contrasts markedly with the austerity of mainland China's restaurants, only a short distance away.

Barbecued Spare Ribs

Preparation Time: 45 minutes **Cooking Time:** 1 hour **Serves:** 4-6

Although Chinese barbecue sauce is nothing like the tomato-based American-style sauce, these ribs are still tasty cooked on an outdoor grill.

Ingredients
4lbs fresh spare-ribs
3 tbsps dark soy sauce
6 tbsps hoisin sauce (Chinese
    barbecue sauce)

2 tbsps dry sherry
¼ tsp five spice powder
1 tbsp brown sugar
4-6 green onions for garnish

First prepare the garnish. Trim the root ends and the dark green tops from the onions. Cut both ends into thin strips, leaving about ½ inch in the middle uncut. Place the onions in ice water for several hours or overnight for the ends to curl up.

    Cut the spare-ribs into one-rib pieces. Mix all the remaining ingredients together, pour over the ribs and stir to coat evenly. Allow to stand for 1 hour. Put the spare-rib pieces on a rack in a roasting pan containing 2 cups water and cook in a preheated 350°F oven for 30 minutes. Add more hot water to the pan while cooking, if necessary. Turn the ribs over and brush with the remaining sauce. Cook 30 minutes longer, or until tender. Serve garnished with the onion brushes.

Top: China requires a vast amount of food to feed its huge population and for this reason farming still occupies four out of five Chinese workers.

Hot & Sour Soup

Preparation Time: 25 minutes **Cooking Time:** 7-8 minutes **Serves:** 4-6

A very warming soup, this is a favorite in winter in Peking. Add chili sauce and vinegar to suit your taste.

Ingredients

2oz pork
3 dried Chinese mushrooms, soaked
   in boiling water for 5 minutes
   and chopped
½ cup peeled, uncooked shrimp
5 cups chicken stock
½ cup bamboo shoots, sliced
3 green onions, shredded
Salt and pepper
1 tbsp sugar

1 tsp dark soy sauce
½ tsp light soy sauce
1-2 tsps chili sauce
1½ tbsps vinegar
Dash sesame seed oil and
   rice wine or sherry
1 egg, well beaten
2 tbsps water mixed with
   1 tbsp cornstarch

Trim any fat from the pork and slice it into shreds about 2-inches long and less than ¼-inch thick. Soak the mushrooms in boiling water until softened. Place the pork in a large pot with the shrimp and stock. Bring to the boil and then reduce the heat to allow to simmer gently for 4-5 minutes. Add all the remaining ingredients except for the egg and cornstarch and water mixture. Cook a further 1-2 minutes over low heat.

Remove the pan from the heat and add the egg gradually, stirring gently until it forms threads in the soup. Mix a spoonful of the hot soup with the cornstarch and water mixture and add to the soup, stirring constantly. Bring the soup back to simmering point for 1 minute to thicken the cornstarch. Serve immediately.

A busy street market in Shanghai. Once little more than a fishing village, it is now one of country's busiest and most overcrowded cities.

Sesame Chicken Wings

Preparation Time: 25 minutes **Cooking Time:** 13-14 minutes **Serves:** 8

This is an economical appetizer that is also good as a cocktail snack or as a light meal with stir-fried vegetables.

Ingredients

12 chicken wings
1 tbsp salted black beans
1 tbsp water
1 tbsp oil
2 cloves garlic, crushed
2 slices fresh ginger, cut into
    fine shreds

3 tbsps soy sauce
1½ tbsps dry sherry or rice wine
Large pinch black pepper
1 tbsp sesame seeds

Cut off and discard the wing tips. Cut between the joint to separate into two pieces. Crush the beans and add the water. Leave to stand.

Heat the oil in a wok and add the garlic and ginger. Stir briefly and add the chicken wings. Cook, stirring, until lightly browned, about 3 minutes. Add the soy sauce and wine and cook, stirring, about 30 seconds longer. Add the soaked black beans and pepper. Cover the wok tightly and allow to simmer for about 8-10 minutes. Uncover and turn the heat to high. Continue cooking, stirring until the liquid is almost evaporated and the chicken wings are glazed with sauce. Remove from the heat and sprinkle on sesame seeds. Stir to coat completely and serve. Garnish with green onions or cilantro, if desired.

Top: street markets play a crucial part in Chinese life, with farmers traveling from outlying areas to sell their produce in the towns.

Crab & Sweetcorn Soup

Preparation Time: 10 minutes **Cooking Time:** 8-10 minutes **Serves:** 4-6

Creamy sweetcorn and succulent crabmeat combine to make a velvety rich soup. Whisked egg whites add an interesting texture.

Ingredients

3½ cups chicken or fish stock
12oz creamed sweetcorn
4oz crabmeat
Salt and pepper
1 tsp light soy sauce

2 tbsps cornstarch
3 tbsps water or stock
2 egg whites, whisked
4 green onions for garnish

Bring the stock to the boil in a large pan. Add the sweetcorn, crabmeat, seasoning and soy sauce. Allow to simmer for 4-5 minutes. Mix the cornstarch and water or stock and add a spoonful of the hot soup. Return the mixture to the soup and bring back to the boil. Cook until the soup thickens. Whisk the egg whites until soft peaks form. Stir into the hot soup just before serving. Slice the onions thinly on the diagonal and scatter over the top to serve.

The Chinese are passionate about good food, believing it is one of the roads to long life, and with an emphasis on fresh vegetables, Chinese cooking is certainly healthy.

Spring Rolls

Preparation Time: 50 minutes **Cooking Time:** 20 minutes **Makes:** 12

One of the most popular Chinese hors d'oeuvres, these are delicious dipped in sweet-sour sauce.

Ingredients
Wrappers
1 cup bread flour

1 egg, beaten

Cold water

Filling
8oz pork, trimmed and finely shredded

¾ cup shrimp, shelled and chopped

4 green onions, finely chopped

2 tsps chopped fresh ginger

4oz Chinese cabbage leaves, shredded

2 cups bean sprouts

1 tbsp light soy sauce

Dash sesame seed oil

1 egg, beaten

To prepare the wrappers, sift the flour into a bowl and make a well in the center. Add the beaten egg and about 1 tbsp cold water. Begin beating with a wooden spoon, gradually drawing in the flour from the outside to make a smooth dough. Add more water if necessary. Knead the dough until it is elastic and pliable. Place in a covered bowl and chill for about 4 hours or overnight.

When ready to roll out, allow the dough to come back to room temperature. Flour a large work surface well and roll the dough out to about ¼-inch thick. Cut the dough into 12 equal squares and then roll each piece out to a larger square about 6 x 6 inches. The dough should be very thin. Cover while preparing the filling.

Cook the pork in a little of the frying oil for about 2-3 minutes. Add the remaining filling ingredients, except the beaten egg, cook for a further 2-3 minutes and allow to cool. Lay out the wrappers on a clean work surface with one corner of each wrapper facing you. Brush the edges lightly with the beaten egg. Divide the filling among all 12 wrappers, placing it just above the front corner. Fold over the sides like an envelope. Then fold over the point until the filling is completely covered, and roll up as for a Swiss roll. Press all the edges to seal well.

Heat the oil in a deep fat fryer or in a deep pan to 375°F. Depending upon the size of the fryer, place in 2-4 spring rolls and fry until golden brown on both sides. The rolls will float to the surface when one side has browned and should be turned over. Drain thoroughly on paper towels and serve hot.

Pot Sticker Dumplings

Preparation Time: 50 minutes **Cooking Time:** 10-20 minutes **Makes:** 12

So called because they are fried in very little oil, they will stick unless they are brown and crisp on the bottom before they are steamed.

Ingredients
Dumpling Pastry
1½ cups all-purpose flour
½ tsp salt

3 tbsps oil
Boiling water

Filling
¾ cup finely minced pork or chicken
4 water chestnuts, finely chopped
3 green onions, finely chopped
½ tsp five spice powder

1 tbsp light soy sauce
1 tsp sugar
1 tsp sesame oil

Sift the flour and salt into a large bowl and make a well in the center. Pour in the oil and add enough boiling water to make a pliable dough. Add about 4 tbsps water at first and begin stirring with a wooden spoon to gradually incorporate the flour. Add more water as necessary. Knead the dough for about 5 minutes and allow to rest for 30 minutes. Divide the dough into 12 pieces and roll each piece out to a circle about 6 inches in diameter.

Mix all the filling ingredients together and place a mound of filling on half of each circle. Fold over the top and press the edges together firmly. Roll over the joined edges using a twisting motion and press down to seal. Pour about ⅛ inch of oil in a large frying pan, preferably cast iron. When the oil is hot, add the dumplings flat side down and cook until nicely browned. When the underside is brown, add about ⅓ cup water to the pan and cover it tightly. Continue cooking gently for about 5 minutes, or until the top surface of dumplings is steamed and appears cooked. Serve immediately.

Special Mixed Vegetables

Preparation Time: 25 minutes **Cooking Time:** 2½-3 minutes **Serves:** 4

This dish illustrates the basic stir-frying technique for vegetables. Use other varieties for an equally colorful side dish.

Ingredients

1 tbsp oil
1 clove garlic, crushed
1 inch piece fresh ginger, sliced
4 Chinese cabbage leaves, shredded
1 cup flat mushrooms, thinly sliced
1 cup bamboo shoots, sliced
3 sticks celery, diagonally sliced
2oz baby corn, cut in half if large

1 small red pepper, cored,
    seeded and thinly sliced
1 cup bean sprouts
2 tbsps light soy sauce
Dash sesame oil
Salt and pepper
3 tomatoes, peeled, seeded
    and quartered

Heat the oil in a wok and add the vegetables in the order given, reserving the tomatoes until last. To make it easier to peel the tomatoes, remove the stems and place in boiling water for 5 seconds. Remove from the boiling water with a draining spoon and place in a bowl of cold water. This will make the peels easier to remove. Cut out the core end using a small sharp knife. Cut the tomatoes in half and then in quarters. Use a teaspoon or a serrated edged knife to remove the seeds and the cores. Cook the vegetables for about 2 minutes. Stir in the soy sauce, sesame oil and seasoning and add the tomatoes. Heat through for 30 seconds and serve immediately.

Top: husking corn in Feng Tai village, Shandong province. Life for Chinese farm workers is an endless struggle to make the land as productive as possible.

Fried Rice

Cooking Time: 5-10 minutes   **Serves:** 6-8

A basic recipe for a traditional Chinese accompaniment to stir-fried dishes, this can be made more substantial with the addition of meat, poultry or seafood.

Ingredients

1lb cooked rice, well drained
    and dried
3 tbsps oil
1 egg, beaten
1 tbsp soy sauce

½ cup cooked peas
Salt and pepper
Dash sesame oil
2 green onions, thinly sliced

Heat a wok and add the oil. Pour in the egg and soy sauce and cook until just beginning to set. Add the rice and peas and stir to coat with the egg mixture. Allow to cook for about 3 minutes, stirring continuously. Add seasoning and sesame oil. Spoon into a serving dish and sprinkle over the green onions.

The Li River has, over millions of years, carved the limestone rocks into strange and beautiful shapes which rise abruptly from the otherwise flat ground.

Cantonese Egg Fu Yung

Preparation Time: 25 minutes **Cooking Time:** 13 minutes **Serves:** 2-3

As the name suggests, this dish is from Canton. However, fu yung dishes are popular in many other regions of China, too.

Ingredients

5 eggs
½ cup shredded cooked meat,
    poultry or fish
1 stick celery, finely shredded
4 Chinese dried mushrooms, soaked
    in boiling water for 5 minutes

1 cup bean sprouts
1 small onion, thinly sliced
Pinch salt and pepper
1 tsp dry sherry
Oil for frying

Sauce

1 tbsp cornstarch dissolved in
    3 tbsps cold water
1 cup chicken stock
1 tsp tomato ketchup

1 tbsp soy sauce
Pinch salt and pepper
Dash sesame oil

Beat the eggs lightly and add the shredded meat and celery. Squeeze all the liquid from the dried mushrooms. Remove the stems and cut the caps into thin slices. Add to the egg mixture along with the bean sprouts and onion. Add a pinch of salt and pepper and the sherry, and stir well.

Heat a wok or frying pan and pour in about 4 tbsps oil. When hot, carefully spoon in about ⅓ cup of the egg mixture. Brown on one side, turn gently over and brown the other side. Remove the cooked patties to a plate and continue until all the mixture is cooked. Combine all the sauce ingredients in a small, heavy-based pan and bring slowly to the boil, stirring continuously until thickened and cleared. Pour the sauce over the Egg Fu Yung to serve.

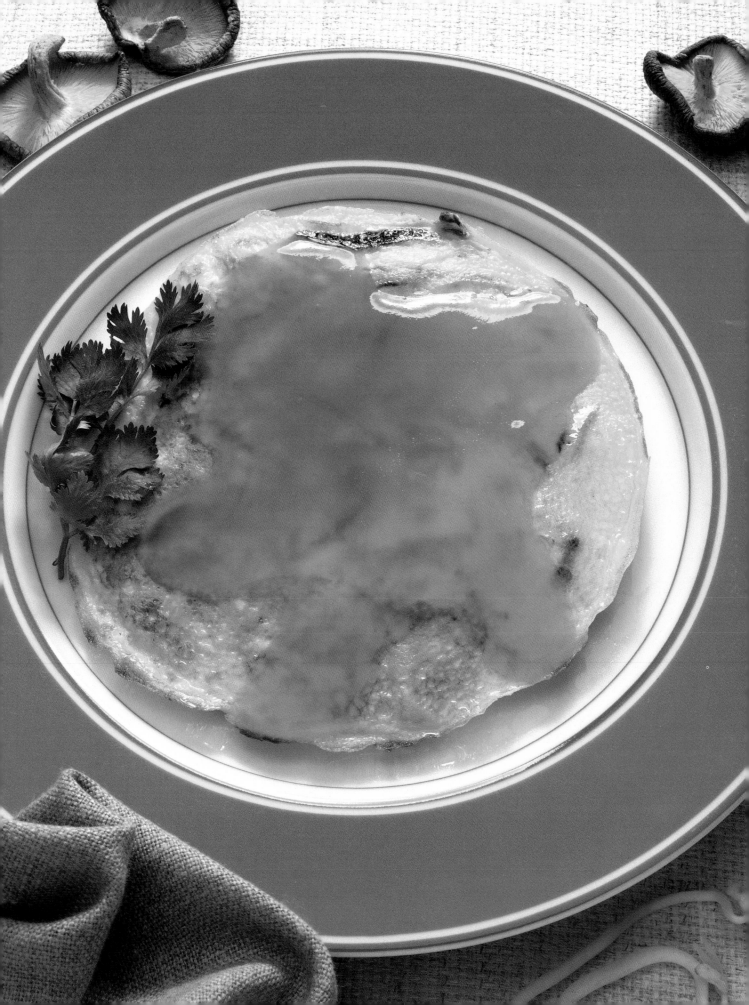

Shanghai Noodles

Preparation Time: 10 minutes **Cooking Time:** 6-8 minutes **Serves:** 4

In general, noodles are more popular in northern and eastern China, where wheat is grown, than in other parts of the country. Noodles make a popular snack in Chinese tea houses.

Ingredients

3 tbsps oil	2 tbsps soy sauce
4oz chicken breast meat	Freshly ground black pepper
4oz Chinese cabbage	Dash sesame oil
4 green onions, thinly sliced	1lb Shanghai noodles, cooked

Heat the oil in the wok and add the chicken cut into thin shreds. Stir-fry for 2-3 minutes. Meanwhile, cook the noodles in boiling salted water until just tender, about 6-8 minutes. Drain in a colander and rinse under hot water. Toss in the colander to drain and leave to dry.

 Add the shredded Chinese cabbage and green onions to the chicken in the wok along with the soy sauce, pepper and sesame oil. Cook about 1 minute and toss in the cooked noodles. Stir well and heat through. Serve immediately.

Top: colorful dancers entertain visitors in Middle Kingdom Park, Hong Kong.

Pork & Shrimp Chow Mein

Preparation Time: 20 minutes **Cooking Time:** 12-14 minutes **Serves:** 4-6

Chinese chow mein dishes are usually based on noodles, using more expensive ingredients in small amounts. This makes economical everyday fare.

Ingredients

8oz medium dried Chinese noodles
1½ cups pork fillet, thinly sliced
1 carrot, peeled and shredded
1 small red pepper, cored, seeded
   and thinly sliced

1½ cups bean sprouts
2oz pea pods
1 tbsp rice wine or dry sherry
2 tbsps soy sauce
1 cup peeled, cooked shrimp

Cook the noodles in plenty of boiling salted water for about 4-5 minutes. Rinse under hot water and drain thoroughly. Heat the wok and add oil. Stir-fry the pork 4-5 minutes or until almost cooked. Add the carrots to the wok and cook for 1-2 minutes. Core, seed and slice the red pepper and add the remaining vegetables, wine and soy sauce. Cook for about 2 minutes. Add the cooked, drained noodles and shrimp and toss over heat for 1-2 minutes. Serve immediately.

A farmer tends his geese in Nanning. Farmers work long and arduous hours, and many are lured to the cities in search of an easier life.

Eggplant & Pepper Szechuan Style

Preparation Time: 30 minutes **Cooking Time:** 7-8 minutes **Serves:** 4

Authentic Szechuan food is fiery hot. Outside China, restaurants often tone down the taste for Western palates.

Ingredients

1 large eggplant
2 cloves garlic, crushed
1 inch piece fresh ginger, shredded
1 onion, cut into 1 inch pieces
1 small green pepper, seeded,
    cored and cut into 1 inch pieces
1 small red pepper, seeded,
    cored and cut into 1 inch pieces
1 red or green chili, seeded,
    cored and cut into thin strips

½ cup chicken or vegetable stock
1 tsp sugar
1 tsp vinegar
Pinch salt and pepper
1 tsp cornstarch
1 tbsp soy sauce
Dash sesame oil
Oil for cooking

Cut the eggplant in half and score the surface. Sprinkle lightly with salt and leave to drain in a colander or on paper towels for 30 minutes. After 30 minutes, squeeze the eggplant gently to extract any bitter juices and rinse thoroughly under cold water. Pat dry and cut the eggplant into 1-inch cubes. Heat about 3 tbsps oil in a wok. Add the eggplant and stir-fry for about 4-5 minutes. It may be necessary to add more oil as the eggplant cooks. Remove from the wok and set aside.

Reheat the wok and add 2 tbsps oil. Add the garlic and ginger and stir-fry for 1 minute. Add the onion and stir-fry for 2 minutes. Add the green pepper, red pepper and chili pepper and stir-fry for 1 minute. Return the eggplant to the wok along with the remaining ingredients. Bring to the boil, stirring constantly, and cook until the sauce thickens and clears. Serve immediately.

Beef with Tomato & Pepper in Black Bean Sauce

Preparation Time: 25 minutes **Cooking Time:** 5 minutes **Serves:** 6

Black beans are a specialty of Cantonese cooking and give a pungent, salty taste to stir-fried dishes.

Ingredients

2 large tomatoes
2 tbsps water
2 tbsps salted black beans
4 tbsps dark soy sauce
1 tbsp cornstarch
1 tbsp dry sherry
1 tsp sugar

1lb rump steak, cut into thin strips
1 small green pepper, seeded
    and cored
4 tbsps oil
¾ cup beef stock
Pinch pepper

Core tomatoes and cut them into 16 wedges. Crush the black beans, add the water and set aside. Combine soy sauce, cornstach, sherry, sugar and meat in a bowl and set aside. Cut pepper into ½ inch diagonal pieces. Heat the wok and add the oil. When hot, stir-fry the green pepper pieces for about 1 minute and remove.

   Add the meat and the soy sauce mixture to the wok and stir-fry for about 2 minutes. Add the soaked black beans and the stock. Bring to the boil and allow to thicken slightly. Return the peppers to the wok and add the tomatoes and pepper. Heat through for 1 minute and serve immediately.

Top: Guilin is one of the most visited areas of China and although it benefits from tourism, farming is still the dominant economic force.

Quick Fried Shrimp

Preparation Time: 30 minutes **Cooking Time:** 2 minutes **Serves:** 4-6

Prepared with either raw or cooked shrimp, this is an incredibly delicious appetizer that is extremely easy to cook.

Ingredients

2lbs cooked shrimp in their shells
2 cloves garlic, crushed
1 inch piece fresh ginger,
   finely chopped
1 tbsp chopped fresh cilantro
   (coriander)

3 tbsps oil
1 tbsp rice wine or dry sherry
1½ tbsps light soy sauce
Chopped green onions to garnish

Shell the shrimp except for the very tail ends. Place the shrimp in a bowl with the remaining ingredients, except for the garnish, and leave to marinate for 30 minutes.

   Heat the wok and add the shrimp and the marinade. Stir-fry briefly to heat the shrimp. Chop the onions roughly or cut into neat rounds. Sprinkle over the shrimp to serve.

The bright lights of Hong Kong attract many Western visitors on their way to the more sedate pleasures of the Chinese mainland.

Sweet & Sour Pork

Preparation Time: 15 minutes **Cooking Time:** 15 minutes **Serves:** 2-4

This really needs no introduction because of its popularity. The dish originated in Canton, but is reproduced in most of the world's Chinese restaurants.

Ingredients

1 cup all-purpose flour
4 tbsps cornstarch
1½ tsps baking powder
Pinch salt
1 tbsp oil
Water
8oz pork fillet, cut into ½-inch cubes
1 onion, sliced
1 green pepper, seeded,
    cored and sliced
1 small can pineapple chunks,
    juice reserved
Oil for frying

Sweet and Sour Sauce
2 tbsps cornstarch
½ cup light brown sugar
Pinch salt
½ cup cider vinegar or rice vinegar
1 tsp fresh ginger, grated
6 tbsps tomato ketchup
6 tbsps reserved pineapple juice

To prepare the batter, sift the flour, cornstarch, baking powder and salt into a bowl. Make a well in the center and add the oil and enough water to make a thick, smooth batter. Using a wooden spoon, stir the ingredients in the well, gradually incorporating flour from the outside, and beat until smooth.

Heat enough oil in a wok to deep-fry the pork. Dip the pork cubes one at a time into the batter and drop into the hot oil. Fry 4-5 pieces of pork at a time and remove them with a draining spoon to paper towels. Continue until all the pork is fried. Pour off most of the oil from the wok and add the sliced onion, pepper and pineapple. Cook over high heat for 1-2 minutes. Remove and set aside.

Mix all the sauce ingredients together and pour into the wok. Bring slowly to the boil, stirring continuously until thickened. Allow to simmer for about 1-2 minutes or until completely clear. Add the vegetables, pineapple and pork cubes to the sauce and stir to coat completely. Reheat for 1-2 minutes and serve immediately.

Chicken Livers with Chinese Cabbage & Almonds

Preparation Time: 25 minutes **Cooking Time:** 4-5 minutes **Serves:** 4

Chicken livers need quick cooking, so they are a perfect choice for the Chinese stir-frying method.

Ingredients

8oz chicken livers
3 tbsps oil
½ cup split blanched almonds
1 clove garlic, peeled
2oz pea pods

8-10 Chinese cabbage leaves
2 tsps cornstarch mixed with
   1 tbsp cold water
2 tbsps soy sauce
½ cup chicken stock

Pick over the chicken livers and remove any discolored areas or bits of fat. Cut the chicken livers into even-sized pieces. Heat a wok and pour in the oil. When the oil is hot, turn the heat down and add the almonds. Cook, stirring continuously, over gentle heat until the almonds are a nice golden brown. Remove and drain on paper towels. Add the garlic, cook for 1-2 minutes to flavor the oil and remove. Add the chicken livers and cook for about 2-3 minutes, stirring frequently. Remove the chicken livers and set them aside. Add the pea pods to the wok and stir-fry for 1 minute. Shred the Chinese cabbage leaves finely, add to the wok and cook for 1 minute. Remove the vegetables and set them aside.

Mix together the cornstarch and water with the soy sauce and stock. Pour into the wok and bring to the boil. Cook until thickened and clear. Return all the other ingredients to the sauce and reheat for 30 seconds. Serve immediately.

Top: rice paddies in Guangdong province. Paddies are still worked mainly by hand with a hoe and spade, or with an ox-drawn plow.

Peking Beef

Preparation Time: 25 minutes **Cooking Time:** 1½ hours **Serves:** 8

In China, meat is often simmered in large earthenware casseroles placed on asbestos mats. A wok is a convenient substitute and the stand does the work of the traditional mat.

Ingredients

2lb joint of beef
1½ cups white wine
2 cups water
2 whole green onions,
   roots trimmed
1 inch piece fresh ginger

3 star anise
½ cup soy sauce
2 tsps sugar
1 carrot, peeled
2 sticks celery
½ mooli (daikon) radish, peeled

Place the beef in a wok and add the white wine, water, green onions, ginger and anise. Cover and simmer for about 1 hour. Add the soy sauce and sugar, stir and simmer for 30 minutes longer, or until the beef is tender. Allow to cool in the liquid.

Shred the remaining vegetables finely. Blanch them in boiling water for about 1 minute. Rinse under cold water, drain and leave to dry.

When the meat is cold, remove it from the liquid and cut into thin slices. Arrange on a serving plate and strain the liquid over it. Scatter over the shredded vegetables and serve cold.

Selling tobacco at the market in Kweilin.

Snow Peas with Shrimp

Preparation Time: 10 minutes **Cooking Time:** 6-8 minutes **Serves:** 2-4

Snow peas, pea pods and mange tout are all names for the same vegetable –
bright green, crisp and edible, pods and all.

Ingredients

3 tbsps oil	2 tsps light soy sauce
½ cup split blanched almonds, halved	¾ cup chicken stock
4oz snow peas	2 tbsps dry sherry
1 cup bamboo shoots, sliced	Salt and pepper
2 tsps cornstarch	1lb cooked, peeled shrimp

Heat the oil in a wok. Add the almonds and cook over moderate heat until
golden brown. Remove from the oil and drain on paper towels. To prepare the
snow peas, tear off the stems and pull them downwards to remove any
strings. If the snow peas are small, just remove the stalks. Add the snow peas
to the hot oil and cook for about 1 minute. Remove and set aside with the
almonds. Drain all the oil from the wok and mix together the cornstarch and
the remaining ingredients, except the shrimp and bamboo shoots. Pour the
mixture into the wok and stir constantly while bringing to the boil. Allow to
simmer for 1-2 minutes until thickened and cleared. Stir in the shrimp and all
the other ingredients and heat through for about 1 minute. Serve immediately.

Top: a repair crew working on the Great Wall. Possibly the greatest man-made
structure on earth, it stretches almost 6,000 kilometres across China.

Sweet-Sour Fish

Preparation Time: 25 minutes **Cooking Time:** 15-25 minutes **Serves:** 2

In China this dish is almost always prepared with freshwater fish, but sea bass is also an excellent choice.

Ingredients

1 sea bass, gray mullet or carp, weighing about 2lbs, cleaned
1 tbsp dry sherry
Few slices fresh ginger
½ cup sugar
6 tbsps cider vinegar
1 tbsp soy sauce

2 tbsps cornstarch
1 clove garlic, crushed
2 green onions, shredded
1 small carrot, peeled and finely shredded
½ cup bamboo shoots, shredded

Rinse the fish well inside and out. Make three diagonal cuts on each side of the fish with a sharp knife. Trim off the fins, leaving the dorsal fin on top. Trim the tail to two neat points. Bring enough water to cover the fish to the boil in a wok. Gently lower the fish into the boiling water and add the sherry and ginger. Cover the wok tightly and remove at once from the heat. Allow to stand 15-20 minutes to let the fish cook in the residual heat.

To test if the fish is cooked, pull the dorsal fin – if it comes off easily the fish is done. If not, return the wok to the heat and bring to the boil. Remove from the heat and leave the fish to stand a further 5 minutes. Transfer the fish to a heated serving dish and keep it warm. Take all but 4 tbsps of the fish cooking liquid from the wok. Add the remaining ingredients including the vegetables and cook, stirring constantly, until the sauce thickens. Spoon some of the sauce over the fish to serve and serve the rest separately.

Fishing on the Li River. The river flows slowly and is often shrouded in mists, lending a languid air to the landscape.

Beef with Broccoli

Preparation Time: 25 minutes **Cooking Time:** 4 minutes **Serves:** 2-3

The traditional Chinese method of cutting meat for stir-frying used in this recipe ensures that the meat will be tender and will cook quickly.

Ingredients

1lb rump steak, partially frozen
4 tbsps dark soy sauce
1 tbsp cornstarch
1 tbsp dry sherry
1 tsp sugar

8oz fresh broccoli
6 tbsps oil
1 inch piece ginger, peeled
    and shredded
Salt and pepper

Trim any fat from the meat and cut into very thin strips across the grain. Strips should be about 3 inches long. Combine the meat with the soy sauce, cornstarch, sherry and sugar. Stir well and leave long enough for the meat to completely defrost. Trim the florets from the stalks of the broccoli and cut them into even- sized pieces. Peel the stalks of the broccoli and cut into thin, diagonal slices. Slice the ginger into shreds. Heat a wok and add 2 tbsps of the oil to it. Add the broccoli and sprinkle with salt. Stir-fry, turning constantly, until the broccoli is dark green. Do not cook for longer than 2 minutes. Remove from the wok and set aside.

Place the remaining oil in the wok and add the ginger and beef. Stir-fry, turning constantly, for about 2 minutes. Return the broccoli to the pan and mix well. Heat through for 30 seconds and serve immediately.

Top: irrigating crops on a commune in Guilin, Guangxi province.

Kung Pao Shrimp with Cashew Nuts

Preparation Time: 20 minutes **Cooking Time:** 3 minutes **Serves:** 6

It is said that Kung Pao invented this dish, but to this day no one knows who he was!

Ingredients

½ tsp chopped fresh ginger
1 tsp chopped garlic
1½ tbsps cornstarch
¼ tsp baking soda
Salt and pepper
¼ tsp sugar
1lb uncooked shrimp

4 tbsps oil
1 small onion, cut into dice
1 large or 2 small zucchini, cut into
    ½-inch cubes
1 small red pepper, cut into
    ½-inch cubes
½ cup cashew nuts

Sauce

¾ cup chicken stock
1 tbsp cornstarch
2 tsps chili sauce

2 tsps bean paste (optional)
2 tsps sesame oil
1 tbsp dry sherry or rice wine

Mix together the ginger, garlic, 1½ tbsps cornstarch, baking soda, salt, pepper and sugar. If the shrimp are unpeeled, remove the peels and the dark vein running along the rounded side. If large, cut in half, place in the dry ingredients and leave to stand for 20 minutes.

Heat the oil in a wok and when hot add the shrimp. Cook, stirring over high heat for about 20 seconds, or just until the shrimp change color. Transfer to a plate. Add the onion to the same oil in the wok and cook for about 1 minute. Add the zucchini and red pepper and cook about 30 seconds.

Mix the sauce ingredients together and add to the wok. Cook, stirring constantly, until the sauce is slightly thickened. Add the shrimp and the cashew nuts and heat through completely.

Chicken with Cloud Ears

Preparation Time: 25 minutes **Cooking Time:** 5 minutes **Serves:** 6

Cloud ears is the delightful name for an edible tree fungus which is mushroom-like in taste and texture.

Ingredients

12 cloud ears, wood ears
    or other dried Chinese
    mushrooms, soaked in
    boiling water for 5 minutes
1lb chicken breasts, boned and
    thinly sliced
1 egg white
2 tsps cornstarch
2 tsps white wine

2 tsps sesame oil
1 cup oil
1 clove garlic
1 inch piece fresh ginger, left whole
1 cup chicken stock
1 tbsp cornstarch
3 tbsps light soy sauce
Pinch salt and pepper

Soak the mushrooms until they soften and swell. Remove all the skin and bone from the chicken and cut it into thin slices. Mix the chicken with the egg white, cornstarch, wine and sesame oil. Heat the wok for a few minutes and pour in the oil. Add the whole piece of ginger and whole garlic clove to the oil and cook for about 1 minute. Take them out and reduce the heat. Add about a quarter of the chicken at a time and stir-fry for about 1 minute. Remove and continue cooking until all the chicken is fried. Remove all but about 2 tbsps of the oil from the wok.

Drain the mushrooms and squeeze them to extract all the liquid. If using mushrooms with stems, remove the stems before slicing thinly. Cut cloud ears or wood ears into smaller pieces. Add to the wok and cook for about 1 minute. Add the stock and allow it to come almost to the boil. Mix together the cornstarch and soy sauce and add a spoonful of the hot stock. Add the mixture to the wok, stirring constantly, and bring to the boil. Allow to boil 1-2 minutes or until thickened. The sauce will clear when the cornstarch has cooked sufficiently.

Return the chicken to the wok and add salt and pepper. Stir thoroughly for about 1 minute and serve immediately.

Singapore Fish

Preparation Time: 25 minutes **Cooking Time:** 10 minutes **Serves:** 6

The cuisine of Singapore was much influenced by that of China. In turn, the Chinese brought ingredients like curry powder into their own cuisine.

Ingredients

1lb whitefish fillets
1 egg white
1 tbsp cornstarch
2 tsps white wine
Salt and pepper
Oil for frying
1 large onion, cut into ½-inch thick
    wedges
1 tbsp mild curry powder
1 small can pineapple pieces,
    drained and juice reserved, or
    ½ fresh pineapple, peeled
    and cubed

1 small can mandarin orange
    segments, drained and
    juice reserved
1 small can sliced water chestnuts,
    drained
1 tbsp cornstarch mixed with juice
    of 1 lime
2 tsps sugar (optional)
Pinch salt and pepper

Starting at the tail end of the fillets, skin them using a sharp knife. Slide the knife back and forth along the length of each fillet, pushing the fish flesh along as you go. Cut the fish into even-sized pieces, about 2 inches. Mix together the egg white, cornstarch, wine, salt and pepper. Place the fish in the mixture and leave to stand while heating the oil.

When the oil is hot, fry a few pieces of fish at a time until light golden brown and crisp. Remove the fish to paper towels to drain, and continue until all the fish is cooked. Remove all but 1 tbsp of the oil from the wok and add the onion. Stir-fry the onion for 1-2 minutes and add the curry powder. Cook the onion and curry powder for a further 1-2 minutes. Add the juice from the pineapple and mandarin oranges and bring to the boil. Combine the cornstarch and lime juice and add a spoonful of the boiling fruit juice. Return the mixture to the wok and cook until thickened, about 2 minutes. Taste and add sugar if desired. Add the fruit, water chestnuts and fried fish to the wok and stir to coat. Heat through 1 minute and serve immediately.

Chicken with Walnuts & Celery

Preparation Time: 20 minutes **Cooking Time:** 8 minutes **Serves:** 4

Oyster sauce lends a subtle, slightly salty taste to this Cantonese dish.

Ingredients

8oz boned chicken, cut into
    1 inch pieces
2 tsps soy sauce
2 tsps brandy
1 tsp cornstarch
Salt and pepper
2 tbsps oil

1 clove garlic
1 cup walnut halves
3 sticks celery, cut in
    diagonal slices
2 tsps oyster sauce
½ cup water or chicken stock

Combine the chicken with the soy sauce, brandy, cornstarch, salt and pepper. Heat a wok and add the oil and garlic. Cook for about 1 minute to flavor the oil. Remove the garlic and add the chicken in two batches. Stir-fry quickly without allowing the chicken to brown. Remove the chicken and add the walnuts to the wok. Cook for about 2 minutes until the walnuts are slightly brown and crisp. Slice the celery, add to the wok and cook for about 1 minute. Add the oyster sauce and water and bring to the boil. When boiling, return the chicken to the pan and stir to coat all the ingredients well. Serve immediately.

In China many crops are still harvested by hand and this back-breaking task is one that has to be endured by almost all members of the family.

Szechuan Fish

Preparation Time: 30 minutes **Cooking Time:** 10 minutes **Serves:** 6

The piquant spiciness of Szechuan pepper is quite different from that of black or white pepper. Beware, though, too much can numb the mouth temporarily!

Ingredients

Chili peppers for garnish
1lb whitefish fillets
Pinch salt and pepper
1 egg
5 tbsps flour
6 tbsps white wine
Oil for frying
2oz cooked ham, cut in small dice
1 inch piece fresh ginger, finely diced
½-1 red or green chili pepper,
   cored, seeded and finely diced

6 water chestnuts, finely diced
4 green onions, finely chopped
3 tbsps light soy sauce
1 tsp cider vinegar or rice wine vinegar
½ tsp ground Szechuan
   pepper (optional)
1 cup light stock
1 tbsp cornstarch dissolved with
   2 tbsps water
2 tsps sugar

To prepare the garnish, choose unblemished chili peppers with the stems on. Using a small, sharp knife, cut the peppers in strips, starting from the pointed end. Cut down to within ½ inch of the stem end. Rinse out the seeds under cold running water and place the peppers in iced water. Leave the peppers to soak for at least 4 hours or overnight until they open up like flowers.

Cut the fish fillets into 2 inch pieces and season with salt and pepper. Beat the egg well and add flour and wine to make a batter. Dredge the fish lightly with flour and then dip into the batter. Mix the fish well.

Heat a wok and when hot, add enough oil to deep-fry the fish. When the oil is hot, fry a few pieces of fish at a time, until golden brown. Drain and proceed until all the fish is cooked. Remove all but 1 tbsp of oil from the wok and add the ham, ginger, diced chili pepper, water chestnuts and green onions. Cook for about 1 minute and add the soy sauce and vinegar. If using Szechuan pepper, add at this point. Stir well and cook for a further 1 minute. Remove the vegetables from the pan and set them aside. Add the stock to the wok and bring to the boil. When boiling, add 1 spoonful of the hot stock to the cornstarch mixture. Add the mixture back to the stock and reboil, stirring constantly until thickened. Stir in the sugar and return the fish and vegetables to the sauce. Heat through for 30 seconds and serve immediately.

Almond Float with Fruit

Preparation Time: 25 minutes   **Serves:** 6-8

Sweet dishes are not often served in the course of a Chinese meal. Banquets are the exception, and this elegant fruit salad is certainly special enough.

Ingredients

1 envelope unflavored gelatin
6 tbsps cold water
$^1/_3$ cup sugar
1 cup milk
1 tsp almond essence
Few drops red or yellow food
   coloring (optional)

Almond Sugar Syrup
$^1/_3$ cup sugar
2 cups water
$^1/_2$ tsp almond extract
Fresh fruit such as kiwi, mango,
   pineapple, bananas, litchis,
   oranges or satsumas, peaches,
   berries, cherries, grapes or starfruit
Fresh mint for garnish

Allow the gelatin to soften in the cold water for about 10 minutes or until spongy. Put in a large mixing bowl. Bring $^1/_3$ cup water to the boil and stir in the sugar. Pour into the gelatin and water mixture and stir until gelatin and sugar dissolves. Add milk, flavoring and food coloring if using. Mix well and pour into a 8-inch square pan. Chill in the refrigerator until set (2 hours).

Mix the sugar and water for the syrup together in a heavy-based pan. Cook over gentle heat until the sugar dissolves. Bring to the boil and allow to boil for about 2 minutes, or until the syrup thickens slightly. Add the almond extract and allow to cool at room temperature. Chill in the refrigerator until ready to use.

Prepare the fruit and place in an attractive serving dish. Pour over the chilled syrup and mix well. Cut the set almond float into 1-inch diamond shapes or cubes. Use a spatula to remove them from the pan and stir them gently into the fruit mixture. Decorate with sprigs of fresh mint to serve.

Sweet Bean Wontons

Serves: 6

Wonton snacks, either sweet or savory, are another popular tea house treat. Made from prepared wonton wrappers and ready-made bean paste, these couldn't be more simple.

Ingredients
15 wonton wrappers
8oz sweet red bean paste
1 tbsp cornstarch

4 tbsps cold water
Oil for deep frying
Honey

Take a wonton wrapper in the palm of your hand and place a little of the red bean paste slightly above the center. Mix together the cornstarch and water and moisten the edge around the filling. Fold over, slightly off center. Pull the sides together, using the cornstarch and water paste to stick the two together. Turn inside out by gently pushing the filled center. Heat enough oil in a wok for deep-fat frying and when hot, put in 4 of the filled wontons at a time. Cook until crisp and golden and remove to paper towels to drain. Repeat with the remaining filled wontons. Serve drizzled with honey.

A magazine vendor smiles proudly for the camera.

Spun Fruits

Preparation Time: 25 minutes **Cooking Time:** 10-15 minutes **Serves:** 4

Often called toffee fruits, this sweet consists of fruit fried in batter and coated with a thin, crisp caramel glaze.

Ingredients
Batter
1 cup all-purpose flour, sifted
Pinch salt
1 egg

½ cup water and milk mixed half
    and half
Oil for deep frying

Caramel Syrup
1 cup sugar
3 tbsps water
1 tbsp oil

1 banana, peeled and cut into
    1 inch pieces
Ice water
1 large apple, peeled, cored and cut
    into 2 inch chunks

To prepare the batter, combine all the batter ingredients, except the oil for deep frying, in a liquidizer or food processor and process to blend. Pour into a bowl and dip in the prepared fruit.

In a heavy-based saucepan, combine the sugar with the water and oil and cook over very low heat until the sugar dissolves. Bring to the boil and allow to cook rapidly until a pale caramel color. While the sugar is dissolving, heat the oil in a wok and fry the batter-dipped fruit, a few pieces at a time. While the fruit is still hot and crisp, use chopsticks or a pair of tongs to dip the fruit into the hot caramel syrup. Stir each piece around to coat evenly. Dip immediately into ice water to harden the syrup and place each piece on a greased dish. Continue cooking all the fruit in the same way. Once the caramel has hardened and the fruit has cooled, transfer to a clean serving plate.

Almond Cookies

Preparation Time: 10 minutes **Cooking Time:** 12-15 minutes per batch **Makes:** 30

In China these are often eaten as a between-meal snack. In Western style cuisine, they make a good accompaniment to fruit or sorbet.

Ingredients

1 stick butter or margarine
4 tbsps granulated sugar
2 tbsps light brown sugar
1 egg, beaten
Almond essence
1 cup all-purpose flour

1 tsp baking powder
Pinch salt
¼ cup ground almonds,
    blanched or unblanched
2 tbsps water
30 whole blanched almonds

Cream the butter or margarine together with the two sugars until light and fluffy. Divide the beaten egg in half and add half to the sugar mixture with a few drops of the almond essence and beat until smooth. Reserve the remaining egg for later use. Sift the flour, baking powder and salt into the egg mixture and add the ground almonds. Stir well by hand. Shape the mixture into small balls and place well apart on a lightly greased baking sheet. Flatten slightly and press an almond on to the top of each one.

    Mix the reserved egg with the water and brush each cookie before baking. Place in a preheated 350°F oven and bake for 12-15 minutes. Cookies will be a pale golden color when done.

Top: the province of Yunnan is poor and sparsely populated, but its warm climate and high rainfall make it perfect for agriculture.

Almond Cookies 68
Almond Float with Fruit 62
Appetizers:
  Barbequed Spare Ribs 12
  Pot Sticker Dumplings 22
  Sesame Chicken Wings 16
  Spring Rolls 20
Barbecued Spare Ribs 12
Beef with Broccoli 50
Beef with Tomato and Pepper in Black Bean
  Sauce 36
Cantonese Egg Fu Yung 28
Chicken Livers with Chinese Cabbage and
  Almonds 42
Chicken with Cloud Ears 54
Chicken with Walnuts and Celery 58
Crab and Sweetcorn Soup 18
Desserts:
  Almond Cookies 68
  Almond Float with Fruit 62
  Spun Fruits 66
  Sweet Bean Wontons 64
Eggplant and Pepper Szechuan Style 34
Fried Rice 26
Fish and Seafood:
  Kung Pao Shrimp with Cashew
    Nuts 52
  Quick Fried Shrimp 38
  Singapore Fish 56
  Snow Peas with Shrimp 46
  Sweet and Sour Fish 48
  Szechuan Fish 60
Hot and Sour Soup 14
Kung Pao Shrimp with Cashew
  Nuts 52
Meat Dishes:
  Beef with Broccoli 50

Beef with Tomato and Pepper in Black
  Bean Sauce 36
Peking Beef 44
Pork and Shrimp Chow Mein 32
Sweet and Sour Pork 40
Peking Beef 44
Pork and Shrimp Chow Mein 32
Pot Sticker Dumplings 22
Poultry:
  Chicken Livers with Chinese Cabbage
    and Almonds 42
  Chicken with Cloud Ears 54
  Chicken with Walnuts and Celery 58
Quick Fried Shrimp 38
Sesame Chicken Wings 16
Shanghai Noodles 30
Side Dishes:
  Cantonese Egg Fu Yung 28
  Eggplant and Pepper Szechuan
    Style 34
  Fried Rice 26
  Shanghai Noodles 30
  Special Mixed Vegetables 24
Singapore Fish 56
Snow Peas with Shrimp 46
Soups:
  Crab and Sweetcorn Soup 18
  Hot and Sour Soup 14
  Wonton Soup 10
Special Mixed Vegetables 24
Spring Rolls 20
Spun Fruits 66
Sweet and Sour Fish 48
Sweet and Sour Pork 40
Sweet Bean Wontons 64
Szechuan Fish 60
Wonton Soup 10